Original title:
Does Life Have a Meaning, or Is It Just a Meme?

Copyright © 2025 Creative Arts Management OÜ
All rights reserved.

Author: Jameson Hartfield
ISBN HARDBACK: 978-1-80566-135-1
ISBN PAPERBACK: 978-1-80566-430-7

Parables in Pixels

In a world of screens that gleam,
We search for purpose, a quirky theme.
With emojis and GIFs, we chart our way,
Yet questioning still, like children at play.

A cat meme laughs, as life unfolds,
With deep thoughts wrapped in pixels bold.
We post our wisdom in bites so small,
Hoping they matter, yet feel so tall.

Serendipitous Suspicion

Awake each day with coffee in hand,
Wondering if all this was truly planned.
Life's a joke that's just too neat,
Like missing the bus, but finding a seat.

We trip on thoughts, like socks in the wash,
Is it fate or folly that makes us posh?
Every stumble, a laugh, in this quirky show,
With questions that swirl, like ice cream and snow.

Beneath the Surface of Smiles

Underneath the smiles we wear bright,
Lies a world of chaos, oh what a sight!
With puns and winks, we navigate fate,
Grinning at shadows, it's never too late.

Why wish on stars when we have a phone?
We meme our wishes, not feeling alone.
Life's a giggle, lost in the fray,
With punchlines tossed, we dance through the day.

Navigating Nonsense

Sailing through nonsense like ships in a storm,
Laughing at logic, it begins to deform.
We paddle through puzzles, with glee in our eyes,
As reason bends out, like escape artist lies.

With snarky one-liners, we chart our space,
Filling the void with a meme-laden grace.
So let's toast to chaos, a fun little rhyme,
In this cosmic comedy, we're lost but sublime.

Playful Paradoxes

In a world of ups and downs,
We dance with silly frowns.
The cat says, 'What's the deal?'
While the dog just wants a meal.

We search for depth in shallow pools,
Debating life with clever fools.
Is the grass just green or blue?
Or is it all a grand debut?

Chasing answers, we often flee,
Tickling fate with glee.
Yet in the mirror, is it true?
A jest or just a peek-a-boo?

In every rhyme, a chance to jest,
Life's a party, if you guessed!
So grab your hat, put on a show,
With a wink, off we go!

Chronicles of the Unseen

Invisible threads weave our days,
Like socks that vanish in a maze.
The chicken laughs, 'What's the punch?'
While pondering if it's lunch.

A squirrel plots, so sly and spry,
Stealing thoughts from passersby.
While ants march on, with tiny dreams,
Absurdity flows like crazy streams.

Time's a wizard in a cloak,
Hiding truths behind a joke.
Each tick and tock, a crafty mime,
Wrinkles thoughts as we unwind.

We gather puzzles, missing piece,
As answers hum, yet never cease.
The unseen world winks with glee,
Mirth and mystery, can't you see?

The Art of Questioning

Why's a banana not a phone?
It can't get calls, it's all alone!
A cupcake asks, 'What's my fate?'
While sprinkles argue—'We're first-rate!'

Quirky queries fill the air,
As goldfish ponder life with flair.
Is there logic in a laugh?
When umbrellas dance, what's the half?

The wise old owl just hoots and spins,
While we trip over cosmic sins.
Should we chase the sun or moon?
Or simply hum an awkward tune?

In every question lies a clue,
An invitation just for you.
The art of asking keeps us bright,
With joy, we dance into the night!

A Nod to the Infinite

In outer space, a pickle floats,
Debating if it's worth the votes.
While comets race for cosmic fame,
And stars giggle—oh, what a game!

A jellybean dreams of being real,
As galaxies twirl, spin, and squeal.
In every twist, a cosmic cheer,
Do we grow old, or just disappear?

Infinity whispers, 'Is it fun?'
While space cats chase the distant sun.
Does laughter echo past our sight?
Or is the joke in endless flight?

So here's a toast to all we see,
To pickles, stars, and jelly, whee!
With every grin and wink so sly,
The universe laughs as it says goodbye!

The Art of Questioning

Why do we look for clues at dawn?
When cats seem wiser than a pawn?
We chase our tails, think it's a sport,
All while the universe hits 'export.'

Are we but shadows in a play?
Or actors lost, led astray?
Banana peels upon the stage,
Slipping through the cosmic haze.

Enigmas Cloaked in Humor.

What if we're just retro tweets?
Echoes of memes on cosmic streets?
A punchline wrapped in endless jest,
Trying to nail down what's the best.

Jokes in the void, where no one hears,
Tickling the fabric of our fears,
Laughter bursts like cheerful rain,
In a world that often drives us insane.

Infinite Echoes

If stars are just clowns in the sky,
Winking slyly as we pass by,
Are we all part of the same scene?
Or jigsaw pieces of a meme machine?

Reflections ripple in a pond,
Where wisdom drifts, lightly donned,
We find our quirks, our silly grace,
In a never-ending cosmic race.

The Search for Significance

What if the answer's all in jest?
A riddle wrapped in a hearty fest?
We try to paint the skies so grand,
While spilling soda on our hand.

In this wild quest for sense and rhyme,
We're just doodles in the sands of time,
Yet we belly-laugh and twirl about,
Finding joy in the absurdity, no doubt!

Journey through a Joke

In a world that spins so fast,
We trip on punchlines that never last.
Chasing wisdom like a fleeting ghost,
We laugh at what we think matters most.

Each riddle wrapped in a silly jest,
Leaves us pondering what feels the best.
Like socks that vanish in the wash,
Life disappears in a comedy posh.

We seek the truth in a rubber chicken,
Yet find our paths are forever stricken.
With giggles echoing through the air,
The meaning hides, we just don't care.

So here we stand, lost in jest,
Finding joy in this grand quest.
If wisdom wears a clownish grin,
Perhaps it's laughter we find within.

Captured in Stillness

Amidst the chaos, there's a pause,
A moment's hush deserves an applause.
Yet in that silence, giggles creep,
Making meaning in our dreams deep.

In quiet corners, punchlines lay,
Waiting for the perfect day.
To spring from shadows, burst to life,
With humor dimming strife and strife.

For stillness holds a comic spark,
Illuminating the inevitable dark.
As we ponder over cups of tea,
Even crumpets giggle raucously.

So let us sit in this still place,
And share a laugh, a warm embrace.
For in this moment, truth takes form,
In silliness, we weather the storm.

The Laughter of Life's Labyrinth

In a maze where logic takes a nap,
We wander through a riddle map.
With every twist, a quip appears,
Spinning wisdom wrapped in cheers.

Every corner hides a playful ode,
Whispering secrets on this road.
As we tumble through this quirky space,
We find joy in the silliest place.

From a mirrored wall, a joke reflects,
Each turn reveals what life neglects.
Tangled up in laughter's thread,
We march on with grins instead.

So grab a friend, let's lose our way,
In riddles bright, we'll laugh and sway.
For in the labyrinth, life's absurd,
Is where we find the deepest word.

The Great Cosmic Chuckle

The universe cracks a fateful grin,
As stardust dances, we spin and spin.
Each quasar winks in the dark of night,
Joking with us in delight's pure light.

Atoms whisper gags in the breeze,
While galaxies twirl with the greatest ease.
They tease us with mysteries so grand,
Yet the punchline's often out of hand.

Black holes sigh with a chuckle deep,
As comets race and the planets leap.
Time twirls round like a merry-goat,
Every tick is a cosmic joke we wrote.

So raise a glass to this vast expanse,
Where meaning's lost in the dance.
For in this chaos, let it be known,
We laugh with the stars, never alone.

The Flirtation of Fate

Is it fate or just a prank,
Life's a joke on some old plank.
We dance with chance, a wobbly fate,
Spin the wheel, oh, isn't it great?

Socks on hands, hats on our feet,
Lessons learned from comic sheet.
We laugh at plans that go awry,
Dare to dream, but just don't try!

Found a fortune in my shoe,
A gum wrapper, shiny and new.
Is luck just banter in the breeze?
Each moment giggles with such ease.

Inquiries float, like paper planes,
Navigating through absurd gains.
Flip a coin, let's take a chance,
Fate's a jester in this dance!

Contemplations in Color

Life's a canvas, splashes bright,
Painting woes with pure delight.
Crayon thoughts in berry hues,
Wondering what today will choose.

Why is grass so green today?
Like the punchlines, they just sway.
Is the bluebird a wise old sage?
Or just another page to gauge?

Rainbows curve like silly jokes,
Dance with clouds, oh how it pokes.
But underneath this playful spree,
Lies a question, full of glee.

So grab your palette, splash away,
Find your joy in shades of play.
In every stroke, a riddle lies,
Humor blooms where laughter flies!

The Absurdity of Being

A rubber chicken on your door,
What's the punchline? Who knows for sure.
Chasing thoughts that fly away,
Like balloons that drift astray.

Quirky hats for serious woes,
Amidst the chaos, humor grows.
Is the universe, in all its might,
Just a prank in the cosmic night?

Pondering life with pie in hand,
Questions float like grains of sand.
Socks and sandals? What a sight!
Fashion choices, pure delight.

In the circus of our days,
Taste the whimsy in your maze.
Absurdities will lead the way,
As we laugh from day to day!

When Jest Meets the Journey

On the road of quirky schemes,
Travel light with silly dreams.
Pack a joke, don't wear a frown,
Life's a carnival, a funny town.

Witty signs along the way,
'Watch for clowns' as if to say.
Imagine life as a grand fest,
With jesters strutting, feeling blessed.

Every bump feels like a laugh,
When we play the silly half.
Riding highs and dodging lows,
With a punchline, the journey flows.

So lift your voice with whimsy's truth,
Celebrate the joy of youth.
In jest we find the sweetest path,
Join the journey, share the laugh!

Searching for Clarity in a Joke

In a world so wide and bright,
I ponder with all my might,
Is there meaning in this jest?
Or just punchlines, like the rest?

I asked a wise old man one day,
He laughed and walked away,
His wisdom, wrapped in riddles tight,
Was lost in giggles, pure delight.

A rubber chicken on my shelf,
Seems smarter than my inner self,
With honks and quacks, it steals the show,
No answers found, but oh, the glow!

So here I stand with silliness,
Embracing life's ridiculousness,
For in the laughs, perhaps we find,
The jests that fill our hearts and mind.

Haikus on Hope

A duck on a lake,
Paddles through dreams, no worries,
Hope quacks in the breeze.

Clouds like cotton balls,
Float away with silly thoughts,
Hope giggles with me.

Starfish on the shore,
Wishing on a cereal,
Hope is breakfast time.

Chickens cross the street,
What's past the road, who can tell?
Hope just likes to walk.

In Search of Substance

I scoured the fridge, what a quest!
For something deep, that's the best,
Found pickles and jam, a curious pair,
Neither could answer with truth or care.

Philosophers with sandwiches grand,
Debating if toast should live or be spanned,
With crumbs on their shirts, they say with cheer,
'Substance is found, right here, never fear!'

I pondered a donut, round and sweet,
A symbol of joy, quite the treat,
But no layers trapped lessons, alas,
Just sprinkles and frosting, not wisdom to pass.

So I laugh in the kitchen, a grand delight,
Stirring up nonsense, by day and by night,
For in the quest for that savory bite,
I find the absurd puts my mind in flight.

Laughter in the Void

In the space between stars, I float,
Lost in thoughts, like a cosmic goat,
Echoes of giggles in the endless night,
A joke told by shadows, pure delight.

Is it just silence, or whispers in air?
Like socks in a dryer, without a care,
I chuckle at nothing, how strange it seems,
Finding punchlines in my midnight dreams.

The void wears a tutu, spins with flair,
Dancing to rhythms of laughter and air,
And though it's a mystery, heavy and dark,
I'll take the giggles over a stark.

So raise a toast to the cosmic jest,
For life's just a riddle, funny at best,
In a universe vast, we weave our tunes,
With laughter as stardust, beneath the moons.

Unraveled Aspirations

Dreams float like balloons, oh so high,
Yet pop like a bubble when you sigh.
Searching for gold at the end of a string,
Just to find it's a cat toy, or some silly thing.

Plans made with glitter, they shimmer and shine,
But often dissolve like a cheap glass of wine.
A compass that spins, oh where is the North?
In the pursuit of success, we just wander forth.

Echoes of Uncertainty

Questions like socks, they go missing in pairs,
Pondering deeply while forgetting my cares.
Are we just actors, on a stage made of cheese?
In this silly drama, we aim to please.

The universe laughs with a cheeky delight,
As we chase after answers that dance out of sight.
When wisdom's a riddle wrapped up in a game,
We giggle together, but who's really to blame?

Joy in the Facade

Wearing a grin that's as bright as the sun,
Hiding the chaos, just for fun.
Life's like a sitcom, with laughter and tears,
We stumble through scripts, forgetting our fears.

Behind every chuckle there's possibly pain,
But who has the time for the mundane's reign?
Let's dance on the edge of a comical fate,
In this ridiculous world, we'll just celebrate!

Searching for the Sacred amidst the Silly

In a world full of memes, where chaos runs free,
We quest for the depth of some cosmic decree.
But amidst all the giggles, a truth might appear,
Hidden in laughter, and washed down with beer.

Wrapped in absurdity, we search for the wise,
Maybe it's covering our skeptical eyes.
As we navigate nonsense, and seek what is real,
Perhaps joy is the meaning, oh what a big deal!

Musing on the Mysterious

In a world of questions, we smile and grin,
Chasing after answers that slip from within.
We ponder our purpose, our grand, noble quest,
While tripping on socks, we're truly the best.

A philosopher stumbles, a giggle erupts,
While searching for truth, he trips on his cups.
With existential musings, we all share a laugh,
As we navigate life, like a half-empty glass.

Between the grand meanings and memes that we weave,
We find it's the laughter that helps us believe.
So let's raise a toast to this joyfully strange,
In the circus of life, it's our thoughts that arrange.

With knock-knock jokes echoing through the abyss,
We ponder the real while we chase after bliss.
So come on and smile, as we wade through the mess,
For the meaning we seek may just wear a red dress.

Unfolding Layers of Laughter

Beneath all the layers, there's giggles and snorts,
Truth wrapped in jokes that the universe courts.
We unravel our thoughts like a ball of old yarn,
Where the punchlines are plenty, and laughter is born.

A sage once proclaimed, with a wink and a tease,
"Life's just a puzzle; don't take it with ease."
So we scratch our heads, sporting big, silly hats,
As we wade through the nonsense, like playful old cats.

The meaning we seek is a riddle of quirks,
Like finding a sock in the laundry that lurks.
Each day is a sketch, with doodles untamed,
Turning profound into memes, oh what fun we've claimed!

As laughter's our language, let's skip and let be,
In the dance of the absurd, we find unity.
So swing, spin, and giggle, till the stars run away,
For in laughter we find the true essence of play.

Serene Chaos

In the calm of confusion, smiles bloom like flowers,
While dancing in circles, we count down the hours.
With chaos our partner, we twirl and we spin,
For the joy in our folly is where we begin.

Why get lost in the chaos when laughs are so near?
We wrestle with life like it's one giant bear.
With each little tumble, we spark up the night,
Turns out the dark holds a glimmer of light!

Whispers of wisdom float through the air,
Like grandmas who joke in their comfy old chairs.
"Life's just a sitcom," they cheer while they bake,
Doughnuts of meaning, for giggling's our take.

So here's to the strangeness, the winks and the grins,
In this serene chaos, where laughter begins.
Through the mess and the muddle, we wade with delight,
For every absurdity? That's our beacon of light!

Voices in the Void

In the depths of the void, echoes call out to play,
With questions like breadcrumbs, they lead us astray.
We ponder the whispers from shadows of thought,
While chuckling at answers that life never brought.

The universe giggles, a cosmic charade,
As we grasp for the truths that continually fade.
In the silence, we find that the joke's always on,
With punchlines that flourish at the break of dawn.

With each little quirk, the cosmos will tease,
While we stumble and fumble like clowns in the breeze.
So let's laugh at the void, embrace its weird charms,
For in this grand riddle, it keeps us from harm.

Amidst all the chaos, the joy is our guide,
In this whimsical dance, we have nothing to hide.
So shout to the silence, let the giggles resound,
In the voices we hear, our laughter is found.

Truths Wrapped in Irony

In life's grand game, we all are players,
Chasing dreams like tired, old slayers.
Wisdom nods, then trips on a cat,
While squirrels discuss life in a top hat.

The universe laughs at our deep thoughts,
Like finding meaning in tangled shoelots.
Philosophers ponder with serious might,
As cats on the windowsill bask in the light.

We wear our regrets like fine silk attire,
Dancing on floors set with dreams of quire.
Yet here we are, stuck in the jest,
Laughing at fate as we talk to the rest.

Irony's wrapped 'round truths like a burr,
A cosmic joke that we all must endure.
So raise your glass to the absurd and the grand,
For life's just a riddle we never quite planned.

The Joy of Ephemeral Moments

A fleeting glance, a grin that's shared,
Moments like gumballs, they're fun and rare.
Ice cream drips on a sunny day,
While thoughts of tomorrow just float away.

We chase the clouds, but they mock our plight,
With rainbows that vanish in the dead of night.
A joke told twice brings laughter anew,
As if life's a buffet, we're all here to chew.

Tickling the timeline, we wiggle and dance,
To a beat that is always out of chance.
Every chuckle's a gem, a fleeting spark,
Like fireflies twinkling in the cool of the dark.

Let's sip our tea beneath the old tree,
And ponder the jokes that we might never see.
For joy's just a snapshot, a flash in the sky,
Let's laugh and forget, then let out a sigh.

Sifting Through the Silly

In a world of logic, I'm lost in the fun,
Like trying to catch a shadow on the run.
Life's like a circus, with clowns and a pie,
You laugh, then you slip, and oh my, oh my!

Searching for wisdom in the bin of odd,
Where rubber ducks and old socks stand in squad.
Each giggle we gather is worth its weight,
Like finding a penny while waiting for fate.

The profound hides away in a jester's cap,
As we scribble our hopes on the back of a nap.
The best of intentions can lead us astray,
Like thinking the toaster will sauté your bay.

So here's to the silly that colors our lives,
To moments of madness, where laughter derives.
In the grand scheme of things, we're all just a spree,
Sifting through chaos, just happy and free.

Where Philosophy Meets Play

On a seesaw of thoughts, we jump to and fro,
What's deep and profound? Oh, who really knows?
With crayons in hand and a smile that's wide,
Let's color the world and enjoy the ride.

Questions like bubbles rise into the air,
Pop! There goes meaning—do we really care?
In the sandbox of life, we build castles tall,
While pondering if we're really here at all.

Banana peels hide where mind games reside,
Slip once or twice, then we'll laugh and abide.
The merry-go-round spins, why not enjoy?
As we find little gems in each silly ploy.

So let's toss our worries right up in the breeze,
Playing our part with the greatest of ease.
In the playground of thoughts, we jump and we sway,
Where philosophy chuckles and joins in the play.

Beneath Clouds of Conundrums

In the circus of thought we spin,
With clowns in their colorful skin.
A question floats like a balloon,
Is it silly or a profound tune?

The jester juggles jokes of fate,
While ducks in a line contemplate.
They quack about wisdom and wit,
But even they're not sure of it.

Mice dance in a maze of cheese,
Exchanging their thoughts with ease.
They nibble on crumbs of delight,
Creating their meanings each night.

So beneath clouds of conundrums high,
Laugh at ducks who just fly by.
Silliness might hold a key,
To unlock the mystery of "be."

The Paradox of Purpose

We ponder at picnics with ants,
Debating if life needs old pants.
A squirrel drops nuts with great flair,
While pondering truth in midair.

The cat naps, blissfully lost,
Dreaming of fish, no matter the cost.
But what of the fish, do they dive?
To wonder if they're just alive?

A turtle shell spins legends bold,
Of heroes and tales that never get old.
Yet the more we spin stories around,
The less of that purpose is found.

But perhaps there's humor in all we twirl,
Like why did the chicken cross, dear girl?
A paradox, where smiles take charge,
Revealing the funny at large!

Ciphers of the Absurd

In shadows of thoughts, the scribbles dance,
With riddle-filled notes and a hint of chance.
A fish in a top hat, sipping its tea,
Mocks the notion of what it could be.

The dog speaks wisdom, or so he claims,
With bark-bark philosophy and riddling games.
While cats plot on rooftops, world domination,
Is it just furry thoughts with no foundation?

Balloons float high, lost in the breeze,
With messages scribbled, "Please get your cheese!"
Absurdity reigns, a carnival scene,
Where logic takes off in a rainbow machine.

So open your mind to the wacky and wild,
Where meaning can scatter, elusive and mild.
For in every giggle and nonsensical word,
Lie secrets of laughter, delightfully absurd!

The Search for Significance

In a world of chaos and cheer,
We scribble questions, loud and clear.
With every laugh and awkward dance,
We ponder fate, as if by chance.

Like cats with yarn, we chase the tail,
Of deeper truths that often fail.
We search for gold in pots of clay,
Yet trip on metaphors each day.

The wise old sage just shrugs and grins,
"Ask a goldfish where time begins!"
The cosmic joke is often missed,
Yet here we are, too fun to resist.

So raise a glass to questions bold,
And toast to stories yet untold.
For in the laughter, life's delight,
We find our path, whether wrong or right.

Scribbles in the Sand

With every wave that comes ashore,
We draw our dreams, then need some more.
Yet tides will laugh and wash away,
Our hopes and fears, in bright decay.

A seagull squawks, a grumpy muse,
While crabs applaud the whimsical views.
"Hey human, quit with all your fuss,
Life's just a game, come join us!"

The grains of sand, they hold our tales,
Of epic fails and legendary trails.
But as we sketch our future's plot,
The wind just sighs, "You've missed the spot!"

So giggle at the universe's jest,
Embrace the mess, it's for the best.
For in the scribbles, short and neat,
We find the fun, a life complete.

Cosmic Jests and Human Hopes

A wink from stars, they've heard our plight,
With cosmic chuckles in the night.
We squint and search for signs divine,
But all we find is pizza signs!

Life's like a joke we're trying to share,
With punchlines hidden everywhere.
We scribble dreams on napkins bright,
Hoping they'll take off in flight.

Yet tumbling thoughts will lead us round,
To wonder if we're lost or found.
But laughter sparkles in the haze,
And guides us through the foggy maze.

So here's to cosmic jesters' games,
With laughter echoing our names.
In the end, the truth we glean,
Is life's a giggle, not routine.

Moments Fleeting, Questions Endless

Tick-tock goes the clock's rude chime,
As we race against the arms of time.
Like fleeting shadows in the light,
We chase the questions, day and night.

A squirrel's dance, a twinge of fate,
We ponder if we've left too late.
With every sip of coffee's brew,
We wonder what's really true.

Yet giggles bubble, rise and swell,
As we embrace the joke we tell.
For in these moments, flash and glee,
We find our meaning, wild and free.

So laugh at worries, let them go,
And join this wacky ebb and flow.
In every question, slight and grand,
We find connection, hand in hand.

The Riddle of Happiness

Why does the cookie jar seem so bright?
Yet the cookies inside are gone without a bite.
I searched for joy in the fridge so deep,
Found only the leftovers, now in a heap.

A clown with a frown, what does he mean?
Juggling life's tasks, what a funny scene!
Laughter is gold, or so they say,
But I'm still stuck with bills to pay.

Chasing my dreams on a pogo stick,
Jumping through life's hoops, does it click?
A dance on the edge of sanity's beam,
Perhaps we're all part of a cosmic scheme.

So here's to the quirks, the smiles we fake,
Happiness hides, like a piece of cake.
We'll laugh till we cry, while we ponder the score,
Is this just a joke, or is there more in store?

Threads of Existence

Spinning my thoughts like a wild ol' cat,
Tangled together, just imagine that!
A sweater of purpose, or just some string?
When I try to wear it, what will it bring?

An onion of meaning, let's peel it right,
Every layer I find brings more awkward fright.
Is it tears of joy, or of utter despair?
With each slice I ponder, do I really care?

Strumming on life's guitar, with one broken string,
Playing tunes of confusion that make my heart sing.
Is it a melody grand, or just pure noise?
Perhaps it's a riddle for lost girls and boys.

So here's to the threads, frayed and yet bright,
We weave and we rumble through day and night.
In laughter we find what it's all about,
A punchline, a wink, and a little doubt.

Echoing in the Abyss

Shouting into the void, what comes back to me?
Just echoes of laughter, or pure misery?
I stumbled upon wisdom in a bottomless pit,
But all I found there was a half-eaten kit.

A mirror reflection, oh what a sight!
Is that my own face, or a ghost taking flight?
I tried to look deeper, but got lost in the glass,
Now I'm stuck pondering what's false and what's brass.

The abyss is funny, with its deep, dark charm,
It tickles your insides and means no harm.
Sipping on chaos like it's the best brew,
Is this what we're doing, or just passing through?

So let's dance in the dark, where most fear to tread,
With laughs that resound, while we scratch our head.
For in the echo, a strange truth parades,
It's all just a punchline, or so it cascades.

Puzzles of Perception

Puzzles scattered 'round like lost socks in the wash,
Each piece I find feels like a grand nosh.
Twist this one, turn that, which way is up?
Life's just a riddle inside a teacup.

A chicken crossed paths, what was its intent?
Was it looking for meaning, or just a fine rent?
Each cluck brings a chuckle, a thought quite absurd,
In the grand scheme of things, what's merely a word?

In a land of denial where dreams go to play,
The sun might shine bright, but it's cloudy today.
I'm tripping over truths, like they're socks on the floor,
Each tangle just whispers, "There's always more!"

So let's giggle at chaos, let's chuckle at fate,
For life, like a joke, comes with some weight.
Finding the humor in every odd twist,
In this grand puzzle, I'd rather not miss.

Vignettes of the Mundane

In the fridge, an empty shelf,
A lone pickle winks at me.
Am I lost in life's great film,
Or just waiting for my tea?

The cat's on a mission bold,
To conquer this cardboard box.
Is he searching for treasure untold,
Or just planning his next socks?

Traffic jams like life's cruel joke,
Bumper stickers sharing faith.
'Honk if you love weird folk,'
Spreads joy like a sunflower wreath.

A sock's missing, oh what a plight,
Wandered off to seek its mate.
In this dance of day and night,
We giggle at life's fickle fate.

Depths of the Undefined

I ponder the cup full of lint,
What truths does it dare to hide?
The vacuum cleaner's on a hint,
Of meanings it won't provide.

An umbrella in July's sun,
Is it shelter or just a jest?
Rain or shine, it's all in fun,
Even if I'm feeling stressed.

Waiter brings the wrong entrée,
"Is that my life on a plate?"
"More salt, please!" I like to say,
As I contemplate my fate.

A plant that thrives, though I forget,
It's surely plotting some grand scheme.
"Water me less!" it seems to fret,
While I'm lost in my wild dream.

Reflections in a Broken Mirror

I looked in shards and saw two heads,
One ponders, the other grins.
"Life's a puzzle," one voice said,
While the other just spins wins.

The toaster pops like a surprise,
"Maybe it's all just a show?"
With burnt bread on the rise,
I laughed; who needs a pro?

A shoe stuffed with another shoe,
In closets of hidden fears.
I ask, "Are you lost too?"
It just squeaks, shedding no tears.

In this carnival of the odd,
Mirrored thoughts bounce back in jest.
Life dances, and we applaud,
While questioning what's for the best.

Laughing at the Void

In the dark of the night, I chuckle,
At the socks that went AWOL.
Did they find a new life to shuffle,
Or just join a grand sock ball?

The fridge hums a low, sweet tune,
As leftovers plot to escape.
"I bet that pie's got a boon,
Let's form a delicious shape!"

Outside, the clouds start to dance,
Fluffy drifters in a delight.
Are they dreaming of a trance,
Or just floating through the night?

With laughter echoing through time,
We chase down the absurd parade.
Is life odd or just sublime?
We giggle, the mysteries fade.

Mirth Amidst the Mysteries

In a world where minds collide,
Questions bounce like bouncing beans.
Is the meaning just a joke?
Or a riddle made of dreams?

Pondering while sipping tea,
Life's an odd parade we see.
Why be serious when you can laugh?
Join the circus, take a gaffe!

Laughter echoes through the halls,
As we trip on mystic calls.
Let's dance with shadows, have some fun,
Wit as bright as morning sun!

All's a play, the stage is set,
In this farce, we won't regret.
So let's embrace the silly ride,
With giggles wide, we'll slip and slide!

Summoning the Specters

In the attic, ghosts convene,
With punchlines sharp and spirits keen.
'What's the point of all this fuss?'
They chuckle, floating without a bus.

A specter says, 'Life's like cheese,
Sometimes stinky, if you please!'
They debate if they should roam,
Or just chill, feeling right at home.

Phantoms whisper with a grin,
Is the fun just built within?
Dance with echoes, spin around,
In this goofy playground found!

'Run from worries, join our spree!
Life's a jest, come laugh with me!'
In the mist, the fun unfolds,
As their tales of whimsy told.

Jests in the Journey

On this winding road we stroll,
With jesters japing, making whole.
Each step forward, what's the score?
Is it treasure, or just folklore?

Knock, knock jokes with every view,
Wit and whimsy, fresh like dew.
Dotting paths with playful spins,
Finding joy in all our sins.

As we tumble, trip and glide,
Life's a game—let's take a ride!
Pack a punchline in your bag,
Unfurl the laughs, don't let them lag!

In the mirrors, funny faces,
Reflecting all our silly places.
So here we are, together still,
In laughter's wake, we climb the hill!

Revisiting the Ridiculous

Once more we gather round the jest,
Each chuckle is a welcome guest.
Returning to the art of fun,
Life's a sketch that's never done.

With rubber chickens at our side,
We banter and we take our stride.
Searching for a punchline bright,
In this whimsical starlit night.

Gags and quips float in the air,
Smile and frown without a care.
All our worries take a leave,
In this craziness, we believe!

So let's toast to the absurd,
With laughter's anthem, let it be heard.
For in each silly little tale,
We find a truth where laughter prevails!

Tales of Time and Meaning

In a world of clockwork ticks,
We search for jokes in cosmic tricks.
Philosophers sip their herbal tea,
While contemplating if cats are free.

The universe shrugs with a grin,
As we ponder where it all begins.
With each tick of the mischievous clock,
We dance to thoughts that tease and mock.

Gravity pulls at our laughter loud,
As we wade through the absurd crowd.
Existence is just a punchline, dear,
Catch the joke, it's already here!

So let's toast with our coffee cups,
To the cosmic jest that fills us up.
In this circus of stars and dreams,
We find our joy in silly schemes.

The Dance of Reality and Riddle

We twirl through time in mismatched shoes,
Playing hopscotch with existential blues.
Reality grins with a cheeky wink,
As we ponder what we really think.

The riddle's wrapped in a rainbow coat,
Where meaning's lost like a silly goat.
We chase our tails in this merry chase,
With questions scribbled on a smiling face.

What's the deal with this cosmic joke?
More twists than a pretzel, it'll make you choke.
Yet laughter bubbles in the midst of tears,
As we spin through the chaos of all our fears.

So dance, oh souls, in the wobbly light,
Of riddles and giggles that feel so right.
In the grand performance, we play our part,
With a wink, a nudge, and a jolly heart.

Sketches of a Transient Life

With crayons and dreams, we sketch our fate,
Each stroke a giggle, never too late.
We scribble on clouds and doodle in sand,
In a world of chaos where we take a stand.

Fleeting moments, like butterflies flit,
We capture them all in a whimsical bit.
In the gallery of what might have been,
Our art of existence is smudged with a grin.

The gallery walls echo our laughter,
As we wander through questions, chasing after.
Is this all, or is there more?
We giggle, we sketch, and explore the core.

So let's paint our woes in colors so bright,
And dance under starlight, embracing the night.
For the transient life is a canvas we share,
With hilarity woven in moments of care.

Wonders in the Whimsical

In a land where the oddballs come out to play,
We ponder the quirks that color our day.
Each thought a balloon, floating on high,
With giggles and gasps that never say die.

Wonders peek from behind every tree,
As life rolls by with a chuckle, you see.
The absurdity sparkles like stars in our eyes,
Where meaning is lost in the dance of the flies.

So let's put on shoes made of laughter and fun,
And cartwheel through sunsets until we are done.
For in this whimsical ride, we all play a part,
With phrases of joy that leap from the heart.

And when the last curtain falls on this show,
We'll giggle together, not feeling the woe.
For in all those wonders, one thing is clear,
The punchline of life is that laughter is near.

Ballads of the Banal

In a world where socks get lost,
And the laundry's always tossed,
We seek the rhyme, the reason why,
As we trip on crumbs and sigh.

Life's a dance with clumsy feet,
Juggling snacks for a laugh, quite sweet,
Like a cat in a cardboard box,
Staring back at life in flocks.

We build our castles made of sand,
Then watch the tide with a comical hand,
Each wave a joke, a jest so grand,
In this playground where we stand.

So cherish the silly, embrace the bland,
With each awkward touch, like a hug so planned,
Life may surprise, in the oddest way,
As we smile at the chaos each day.

Moments in a Mirthful World

A pancake flops off the plate,
Bounce and roll—it's set on fate,
Syrup rivers make me laugh,
As I seek the perfect half.

The crossword fill can make us grin,
As we puzzle out where to begin,
Each letter's dance in playful sway,
In a mind game that leads astray.

Then there's the cat with glasses on,
Strutting 'round like it's the dawn,
With a flick of its tail, a pose, a purr,
Claiming moments, all that occur.

In this delightful, funny sphere,
Each little hiccup we hold dear,
For life's a jest, a playful whirl,
In the fabric of this quirky world.

Between Giggles and Gloom

Step through a door to the unknown,
Where shadows dance, but laughter's grown,
We fumble through the ups and downs,
Painting joy with goofy frowns.

Like a chicken in a fowl parade,
Waddling along, a funny charade,
We find our roles in the grand display,
As mishaps lead the merry way.

Balancing troubles on wobbly stilts,
While life's absurd in its quirky quilts,
Each blunder's a stitch in time's great seam,
As we wade through this charming dream.

So giggle at gloom, don't shy away,
For each stumble brings a brighter day,
In the space between, we learn to play,
Creating laughter from disarray.

The Playful Nature of Truth

The truth is often a sneaky tease,
With riddles scattered like autumn leaves,
It wears a hat, sometimes a clown,
Mischieving as it jumps around.

Like a duck that quacks in a gentle breeze,
While planting smiles with every sneeze,
It flutters by with a wink and nod,
Turning wisdom into a whimsical prod.

In gardens of insight, truths may sprout,
But they're often tangled in playful doubt,
Each answer hides in a giggly frown,
As we chase it merrily up and down.

So let's toast the truth with a slice of pie,
With laughter ringing as we pass it by,
For the best of knowledge wears funny shoes,
And walks the line of giggles and blues.

Navigating the Unknown

With a map that's blank and wide,
I search for joy in every tide.
The compass spins, is it a prank?
Or am I drifting into the dank?

I asked a seagull, 'What's the plan?'
It just squawked, flew off like a fan.
The stars above, in a twinkly game,
Are they guiding me, or just to blame?

In the café, a cup of brew,
I ponder skies of pink and blue.
Are clouds just fluff or dreams we chase?
Or maybe just a cosmic vase?

So here I stand with laughter stout,
In the absurdity, I snooze and shout.
With giggles wrapped in cosmic foam,
Who knows, maybe this chaos is home!

A Comedian's Compass

With punchlines poised like arrows sharp,
I juggle thoughts in the cosmic harp.
Each giggle echoes a question or two,
Is this a joke, or is it true?

I crack a smile at life's grand scheme,
While finding humor in every dream.
When life's a stand-up, I take the stage,
And laugh at fate, it's all the rage!

A banana peel, I slip and slide,
Through slips of meaning, oh what a ride!
With every quip, I may just find,
The punchlines formed in space and time.

So forth I go with a wink and nudge,
In the comedy of life, I won't budge.
With laughter's light, I'll roam the night,
For the bizarre feels pretty right!

The Quirks of Existence

In a circus tent of strange, we play,
Life's a riddle in every way.
I wear my hat at a crooked tilt,
Chasing giggles with no guilt!

A goldfish muses, 'What's the score?'
As I debate with spoons galore.
Do socks get lost or join a band?
I swear they're plotting, isn't that grand?

With a wink at fate and a twirl of fate,
I ponder why we hesitate.
Do clocks run fast, or do they stall?
Tick-tock, tick-tock, hear the call?

So let's embrace the quirks we own,
In the wackiest journey, we've ever known.
With laughter as our trusty guide,
We'll dance through life, let fun abide!

Daydreams of a Drifting Soul

In clouds of cotton and dreams on sail,
I drift through thoughts, a whimsical trail.
With giggles tucked in my pocket tight,
I sail on whimsy, daydreams take flight!

What makes the sun rise with a grin?
Is it just playing, or is it a win?
While shadows dance and chuckles bloom,
In this odd world, I find my room.

My shadow whispers, 'Let's jest and play,'
As I sway along in a silly ballet.
With every chuckle, I break the mold,
In the theatre of life, where humor's bold.

So, here I drift with delight and whim,
In the sailboat of laughter, I'll never swim.
For in these daydreams, so brightly spun,
I find my meaning, all wrapped in fun!

The Weight of Whimsy

In the circus of existence, we prance and sway,
Chasing after questions that tease and play.
Wearing mismatched socks, we dance in the rain,
Hoping for wisdom, but giggling in vain.

Every thought is a jester, dressed in a frown,
Reflecting on moments, we tumble down.
Life's a grand riddle wrapped in a jest,
An enigma we treasure, yet never can test.

So we juggle our worries, on a unicycle ride,
Wobbling on answers we dare not decide.
The meaning's a banana, all squishy and bright,
Slipping on wisdom, we laugh at our plight.

With a wink to the cosmos, we tip our hats,
Celebrating nonsense with umbrella bats.
In the garden of giggles, we plant our dreams,
Frolicking merrily, bursting at the seams.

Bridging the Gap of Gloom

Between the shadows where thoughts like to creep,
We build a fine bridge, but it's shallow and steep.
With each silly step, we might tumble and flop,
Yet grins keep us going, we ain't gonna stop.

We ponder and wonder, like cats in a hat,
Searching for answers while stuck in a spat.
Life's a puzzle that rarely fits right,
Yet we laugh through the chaos, finding joys in the fight.

With quizzical nods and a wink of the eye,
We toast to the maybes that swirl in the sky.
For every profound thought that might drift on by,
There's a rubber chicken lurking just to pry.

So we'll dance through the gloom, with a wink and a spin,

Embracing the wacky in all we begin.
With laughter as armor, we're ready to play,
Bridging the gaps in a humorous way.

Between Laughter and Reflection

In the realm of the pondering, where thoughts like to dance,
We grapple with questions, yet take our chance.
With a chuckle as armor and laughter our sword,
We battle the serious, we're never bored.

Between giggles and musings, a tightrope we tread,
Wobbling on wonder, while chuckling ahead.
Why summon the frown when we can just smile?
Let the wisdom be playful, let joy be our style.

For life is a joke that twists like a vine,
With punchlines connecting like stars that align.
In a sea full of what-ifs and maybe one days,
We'll sketch silly scenarios, in colorful ways.

So here's to the laughter that helps us escape,
The serious burdens, the dreary landscape.
With each quirky thought, we raise up our cheer,
In the heart of the nonsense, life's meaning is here.

Silhouettes of Sentience

In a world full of chatter, we sift through the noise,
Finding joy in the quirky, like children with toys.
Each thought is a silhouette against the night,
Casting shadows of wisdom, yet dancing in light.

We ponder the reasons that brought us to be,
With giggles and snickers like drops from a tree.
Life's just a canvas where silliness spreads,
Painting giggle-fueled tales inside our heads.

As we tread through the mysteries wrapped up in a dream,
We carry our laughter like ice cream to scream.
Though shadows may linger, we choose to embrace,
The whimsical whispers that tickle our face.

So let's twirl in the moonlight, our giggles a guide,
Navigating existence, with nonsense as pride.
For in each goofy moment, we'll find what we seek,
A glimpse of the meaning that makes our hearts peek.

The Essence of Being

In a world where socks can't find their mate,
We search for answers, a curious fate.
Chasing our tails in a circle so wide,
Laughing at wisdom we just can't abide.

Cats on the keyboard know something we don't,
Their purrs contain secrets that flicker and fawn.
We sip on our coffee, our brows in a frown,
Wondering why we just twirl around.

Fish that pretend to be swimming in air,
Asking us questions, but do we even care?
The trees hum a tune that we can't quite catch,
While ants hold a party, we quickly dispatch.

Life is a circus, or maybe it's not,
Clowns at the door, but we've got a plot.
So let's hold our noses and jump in the fray,
If there's meaning, it's dressed in a funny bouquet.

Dancing with Absurdity

A penguin in a tux, what a sight to behold,
Strutting through life, both funny and bold.
With every odd twirl, he flips the routine,
As we laugh at the chaos, we're caught in a dream.

The moon winks at rabbits who wear silly hats,
As they plot their next moves, with some cheeky chats.
While fish serenade in their rainbowy bling,
We sip on our lattes, embracing the zing.

Life's like a joke with the punchline unknown,
While we scramble and giggle, we're never alone.
Embrace all the quirks, let the nonsense be free,
In this dance of absurd, we find pure glee!

So bring on the weird, let's revel in fun,
With every snicker, a new day's begun.
In the heart of the jest, when we'll laugh till we cry,
We'll find meaning in moments that just pass us by.

Between the Lines of Reality

In the space where rainbows and salads collide,
We ponder the truth while wearing a slide.
With whimsical whimsies that tickle the brain,
We juggle our thoughts like a circus of grain.

A toaster for thoughts, a kettle for dreams,
We sip on our whimsy and burst at the seams.
As colors concoct in a vibrant display,
We dance with our questions, 'What on earth did they say?'

The cat with its wisdom, a crown on its head,
Dictates our moments with yarn in its tread.
We chuckle at time slipping through our fingers,
As if it were cheese, that forever just lingers.

Between each absurdity, truth hides itself,
Like a book on the shelf that no one will help.
So let's read between laughter, in silliness sway,
For meaning is muddled but never cliché!

Shadows of Certainty

In shadows where certainty skips and it hops,
We find all the answers wrapped up in some flops.
The chicken debates with a wise old hen,
While clouds turn to bunnies, 'Are we sure, or again?'

Puzzles unraveled by a puzzling fox,
Who dances in circles, unfastening locks.
Catch my drift—oh wait, is it a meme?
These shadows remind us, it's all a big scheme.

The lamp post is whispering secrets at night,
While stars twinkle sass, pushing wrongs into right.
And giggles explode from a worm in a tie,
As we ponder the meaning, just too sly to deny.

With emojis and laughter, the truth hides in glee,
Winking at questions with a silly decree.
So come on, embrace all the quirky delight,
For shadows show certainty in nonsense so bright.

Reflection in a Cracked Mirror

In the glass, I see my face,
A jigsaw puzzle, out of place.
Each crack a story, wild and grand,
A riddle written in shifting sand.

I smile at hints of wisdom's glow,
But giggle at what I do not know.
Like a joke with no punchline in sight,
Life's a riddle in morning light.

Do I trip on thoughts too deep to tread?
Or jump for joy with a nod to dread?
With every laugh, the truth eludes,
Just a punchline made for fools and dudes.

So here's a toast to the quirky riff,
Of who we are and all our schiff.
Embrace the strange, the silly, the fun,
In this fractured world, we all are one.

Chasing Shadows of Meaning

I chased a shadow down the lane,
It giggled madly, but felt no pain.
I asked it kindly for a clue,
It winked and said, 'That's up to you!'

So I pranced and danced in circles tight,
While pondering day and dreaming night.
Each thought a balloon, soaring high,
Then popped by laughter, oh my, oh my!

The deeper I dived, the less I found,
But oh, how I twirled on the ground!
With sneakers worn and hair askew,
Life's a circus; and who's the fool?

So if you find you're lost at sea,
Just tickle the waves; be wild and free.
Like a shadow show in a quirky play,
Meaning's just a laugh away!

Fragmented Narratives

Once upon a time, or so they say,
A goat danced wildly, full of play.
His story broke before the thrill,
Yet laughter echoed, never still.

In chapters lost, we find our roles,
Like socks misplaced in laundry trolls.
Each tale a giggle, each laugh a tear,
Life's just a sitcom, far and near.

In fragmented dreams, we seek the thread,
Twisting and turning, where angels dare tread.
So grab a quill and scribble fast,
For meaning's just a fleeting blast!

In this wild script we play our part,
With winks and nudges, and a dash of art.
So take a bow, embrace the scene,
For every comic has a gleam!

The Meme of Being

In a world of pixels and funny glares,
We scroll through life without a care.
Each meme a giggle, each laugh a thread,
We dance and tumble, never dread.

With filters bright and faces bent,
We meme our truth, or just pretend.
Life's a canvas, splattered with cheer,
In every joke, our tale is clear.

So come and poke at the big unknown,
With a rubber chicken and a silly drone.
In laughter's arms, we may just find,
The secret to life's giggly grind.

So here we are, in this grand parade,
Balloons of nonsense, never afraid.
Join the fun, embrace the jest,
For in being meme, we're truly blessed!

Reflections of the Ridiculous

In a world of goofy dreams,
Laughter's the glue, or so it seems.
We chase the joke, we miss the point,
Life's a punchline in a jester's joint.

With hats like cats and shoes on hands,
Reality juggles our wild demands.
But who knew socks could dance so well?
In this circus, we cast our spell.

The mirror cracks, we grin wide,
We're clowns with secrets, we mustn't hide.
Tickles of wisdom in every jest,
In a world of nonsense, we're truly blessed.

So let's toast to the absurd spree,
A life where nonsense flows free.
For when the punchline's the only thread,
We find euphoria in laughter instead.

A Tapestry of Tension and Tickle

A tapestry woven of giggles and sighs,
Life's fabric is frayed, with each silly tie.
With threads of chaos and knots of fun,
We dance on the edge of a punsy run.

Tickle my fancy, I'm ready to roll,
In this play we call life, humor's the goal.
When the serious slips and falls on its face,
We'll wrap it in humor, make it a race.

Each day a riddle, a joke or a pun,
Why take it too seriously? Let's just run!
In the pockets of time, where absurdity thrives,
We craft our delight and see how it vibes.

A canvas of laughs that cushions our fears,
With a splash of whimsy, we'll paint the years.
So let's weave it together, the strange and the neat,
For a tapestry folded in laughter's heartbeat.

Explorations in Euphoria

In the land of the silly, we tread with glee,
A map drawn to laughter, that's the key.
Searching for joy in the most bizarre,
Like chasing a comet or imagining a star.

We climb on the backs of giggling whales,
Sailing through life with ridiculous tales.
Beyond the horizon, where absurdities lie,
We'll ride on the winds of a pie in the sky.

With each ludicrous twist, there's wisdom to gain,
We twirl like ribbons in a soft summer rain.
In the wackiest dreams, fears come undone,
As we dance under starlight, laughing till we're spun.

So let's celebrate joy in all its strange forms,
Seeking laughter like treasure through life's wild storms.
For in every zany adventure we see,
Is the blossoming peace of what it means to be free.

Glimpses of Giggles

In paths where the silly and strange intertwine,
We find glimmers of joy in a glass of wine.
With wobbly steps and a wink of the eye,
Life's a funny quirk, and oh my, why not try?

The awkward moments can spark the delight,
When the penguin wobbles into the night.
Each stumble's a story, each fall a surprise,
In the comedy club of our worldly lives.

So here's to the mishaps, the blunders in cheer,
To laughter that echoes, sincere and near.
Let's savor the fun, forget all the strife,
For a giggle a day keeps away all the blife!

The snippets of joy in the grand parade,
In a world of absurd, we won't be dismayed.
So, grab your hats, and let's leap into dreams,
In the glimpses of giggles, life's more than it seems.

Reality's Riddle

Why do we chase a golden prize,
With peanut butter stuck to our thighs?
A hamster wheel spins, oh, so bright,
While we ponder our place in the night.

We juggle dreams like clown-shaped balloons,
And gaze at the stars while humming old tunes.
The point of it all seems like a jest,
As we laugh and complain, forgetting the rest.

A cat falls down, lands on its feet,
While we trip over socks in the street.
Is it fate or some cosmic joke?
As laughter erupts over breakfast smoke.

So here we stand, in a cosmic queue,
Eating cold pizza while sipping on brew.
Perhaps in this dance of the wild and absurd,
We'll find meaning, or maybe just dessert.

Dance of the Absurd

Twirl in your pajamas, let's start a parade,
With mismatched socks—it's all been laid.
The universe giggles at our silly plight,
As we salsa with shadows in the dim evening light.

The fridge hums softly, a chef's hidden glee,
Whispers of leftover mystery.
We serve soup from a jar, it's a gourmet affair,
While napkins serve as our sartorial flair.

A rubber chicken in a serious debate,
Makes existential claims while we contemplate fate.
The meaning of life, a jesters' decree,
Is wrapped up in laughter and a hot cup of tea.

So dance with a giggle, embrace the unknown,
In a world of quirks, you won't be alone.
Maybe the answer is tucked in a pun,
Where joy and absurdity secretly run.

Threads of Fulfillment

In the tapestry, we weave day by day,
With threads of chaos in a colorful array.
But the needle keeps dropping, our patience is thin,
As we sip from the cup where our wild dreams begin.

Each stitch a blunder, a laugh off the track,
With tangled yarn giving our purpose some flack.
We craft our own motto: 'What do we know?'
As we ponder our worth in a threadbare tableau.

The wise old owl says, "Just knit and unwind,"
While a squirrel in a tie claims it's all in your mind.
We barter our quirks for some simple delight,
Finding gold in the odd, shining bright through the night.

So let's not despair at our lopsided seam,
As the fabric of life begs us to dream.
In the threads of fulfillment, let giggles unfurl,
Life's odd little joys give our hearts a whirl.

The Irony of Existence

A toaster gives order, pops bread into space,
While we contemplate meaning with crumbs on our face.
The kettle starts whistling, it knows what it's doing,
While we sit in a circle of pondering ruin.

A chicken crossed roads, quite absurdly, it seems,
To escape the deep questions, the endless daydreams.
In pants that don't fit, we dance like a fool,
As the irony lands with the weight of a mule.

We juggle our worries like flaming torches,
With the sun in our eyes, we squint through the corridors.

We ask for the answers while writing our scripts,
Yet the punchline arrives when we least expect it.

So raise up your glass, toast the cosmic surprise,
To the irony-knitters of life's wacky ties.
For in laughter and mayhem, we find our own song,
In this curious dance, where we all belong.

Existential Echoes

In a world of noise, I ponder and play,
Is this all a joke, or a serious buffet?
A banana peel slip, I laugh in despair,
As deep thoughts collide with a well-placed air.

Questions parade like clowns in my mind,
Each one a jest, each punchline unkind.
I trip and I tumble, a cosmic ballet,
Searching for answers while the universe sways.

The stars wink in jest, what's the point, they say,
"Dance like a fool, it's a grand cabaret!"
I join in the fun, throwing logic aside,
Bowtie on my thoughts, let absurdity ride.

So here's to the chaos, the giggles we seek,
With breadsticks of wisdom and humor unique.
We're all just a meme, a joke made of light,
In this cosmic circus, let's laugh through the night.

The Paradox of Purpose

A chicken crossed the road for a reason unclear,
Seeking the meaning, or a cold pint of beer?
With each step it took, the plot thickened quite thick,
Was it searching for purpose, or just playing a trick?

Life's a riddle wrapped in a punchline or two,
Where every deep answer just leads back to goo.
The wise men all nod, with their beards and their charms,
While I juggle my questions with existential alarms.

"Why are we here?" I ask of a cat,
It looks back and meows, "You're just overreact."
Chasing my tail, what a whimsical scene,
Maybe purpose is found in the places we've been.

So cheers to the jesters, the jest that we play,
With each silly stumble, we brighten the day.
Life's a paradox, wrapped in a pun,
Embrace the absurd, we're all part of the fun.

Whispers in the Void

In the silence I hear, a whimsical hum,
Are thoughts just balloons, or are they bubbles of gum?
With voices of jester, they whisper and tease,
"Find meaning in laughter, or just do as you please!"

The void echoes back with a chuckle or twang,
A symphony of giggles that funnily sang.
Each quirk of existence a dance in disguise,
Where nonsense blooms brightly and wisdom just sighs.

A squirrel on a branch wears a philosopher's hat,
Asking deep questions while he chases a rat.
"Is this all there is?" as he leaps in the air,
Sometimes we find answers in a whimsical flare.

So I ponder in jest, as I stretch to the sky,
With cotton candy thoughts that just float on by.
In whispers and giggles, a truth soft and coy,
Life's meaning is laughter—it's our greatest joy!

Laughter in the Abyss

Into the abyss, I peer with a grin,
A void full of whispers, where giggles begin.
Do shadows have secrets, or do they just nap?
I'm betting they dream in a cosmic mishap.

With each tumble down, there's a joke waiting there,
A pun on the edge, floating free in the air.
As I dance with the echoes, a footstep away,
From realizing folly is the price we all pay.

The abyss starts to chuckle, as it swallows my fate,
"Life's but a jest, and you're just my mate."
So I twirl and I spin, in this cosmic charade,
Finding giggles in ruins, in the mess we have made.

Together we laugh, spirit and cheer,
In the depth of the void, there's just nothing to fear.
For amid all the questions, absurd and profound,
The laughter in the abyss makes joy ever abound.

Whispers of Existence

Under the stars, we ponder and laugh,
Is it all a game, or just some giraffe?
Chasing our tails in a cosmic ballet,
Finding deep meaning in cabbages? Hey!

Life's like a puzzle, with pieces that shift,
One moment it's bliss, then a particularly bad gift.
We dance on ideals, like clumsy old fools,
Asking if wisdom is written in drools.

Yet here we are, munching on cake,
Wondering if truth is a method of bake.
A slice of existence, topped with some cream,
Perhaps it's just laughter, a whimsical dream.

So we sip our drinks, with a wink of fate,
While debating if 'exist' is just one big plate.
With humor as sauce, we're never alone,
In this riotous feast, we're finally home.

Perhaps a Fleeting Thought

What is this life, a wild little shindig?
A dance with the cosmos, or just a small fig?
We giggle at wisdom, try to put on a face,
But all we can find is last week's disgrace.

Ideas come floating on balloons made of air,
They pop with a laugh, do we really care?
A thought that was deep, now just a mere blip,
Like tickles from fate, on a joyride trip.

So we chuckle at purpose, as it runs in a race,
With wobbly old legs, it's lost in the space.
But if life is a jest, then we're the punchline,
Served with a grin, and a glass of good wine.

Let's toast to the questions, let's grin through the chase,
For perhaps our small joys are the ultimate grace.
Life may be fleeting, but humor endures,
Fleeting or firm, it sure entertains yours!

When Laughter Meets Mortality

Knock, knock on death's door, can I let you in?
I'm busy deflecting this proverbial fin.
With puns and with punchlines, I dance in the gloom,
If the grave's a big stage, watch me claim my room.

Witty comedies play on the edge of our fate,
We laugh till we cry as we contemplate.
In this grand little theater, we take our last bow,
With a wink and a chuckle, oh what a wow!

The meaning may hide, like a cat in a box,
Behind all our jokes, or just some bad socks.
But heck, life's for living, with humor our shield,
In the battle with time, laughter's the field.

So here's to the giggles, the gaffes, and the fun,
As we whirl through existence 'til we all come undone.
If laughs are the currency, I'll be a rich brat,
Rolling through life with a joke and a hat!

Fragments of Purpose

In the search for a meaning, we stumble and trip,
Like a clown on a tightrope with a pie on his lip.
We're fragments and puzzle pieces, lost in a dream,
Trying to fish for a purpose in an ocean of cream.

With the world as our stage, we juggle our fate,
Dancing in circles while we contemplate.
Each chuckle a treasure, each giggle a clue,
In this riddle of life, the punchline is you.

So we toss our confetti as the questions unfold,
Celebrating the moments, both awkward and bold.
Perhaps we're the jesters, with hearts full of cheer,
Building our meaning, one laugh at a year.

So scrap all the scripts and just go for the ride,
With humor our guide, let's enjoy the glide.
For in fragments of laughter, we gather our peace,
The meaning of life—let it tickle, increase!

www.ingramcontent.com/pod-product-compliance
Lightning Source LLC
Chambersburg PA
CBHW072146200426
43209CB00051B/759